HAPPY
WARRIOR
JOURNAL

Live a Life you Love

Hardcover ISBN: 978-1-7345276-3-6

Library of Congress Control Number: 2021907334

Note from the Authors

Happy Warrior,

We're excited you're here.

We are NYU-certified coaches, authors, speakers, and happiness experts with over two decades of coaching experience between us. We met in a marketing class at NYU where we were both pursuing our coaching dreams. We joined forces shortly after, in 2013, to create Selfscription® Mindset, a coaching journey and workbook, which we have been using with our private clients for several years. We are now bringing these powerful tools and practices to you.

Through many ups and downs, starts and stops, we persevered. In 2018, Selfscription® expanded to feature articles, a notebook collection, and other products designed to take your happiness journey to the next level. On March 20, 2020, The International Day of Happiness, we published our groundbreaking book, Happy Warrior - Empower Your S.E.L.F. in 30 Days - Your Practical Guide to a Happy Life.

We wish to dedicate this Happy Warrior Journal to both of our families, friends, clients, and guides who continue to love and support us on this great adventure.

Of course, none of this would be possible without the power of love to conquer fear.

Choose Love,

John & Jami

What does it mean to be a Happy Warrior?

Happiness is not just a feeling; it's a mindset and a way of life. It means making a choice to accept and be grateful for ourselves and the people around us. It means that we choose to be purposeful and thoughtful in all areas of our lives. And it means that we are choosing to see how life might actually be happening *for* us, instead of *to* us.

A Happy Warrior is a person who navigates life with intention, kindness, and courage. A Happy Warrior fights the good fight of choosing love over fear, over and over again. Choosing to operate from love is simple, but not easy. The further a Happy Warrior travels on their journey, the more elaborate the life lessons become. A Happy Warrior doesn't give up; they keep growing and evolving.

Happy Warriors travel through life gently; they don't force life to happen. Instead, they allow life to unfold. They listen to their heads and their hearts and make decisions based on logic, as well as what feels right inside of them. Happy Warriors experience the challenges of life just like everyone else, but they handle the challenges, feel their feelings, and they make happiness and love their true north.

Happiness is not something we can buy or sell, and it's not acquired through a particular accomplishment or event. Happiness is inside each one of us and can be ours at any moment when we decide to embrace it. There is plenty of Happiness for everyone; it never runs out. Happiness is a choice. And the choice is yours.

This is what it means to choose happiness. This is what it means to empower yourself and walk the path of a Happy Warrior.

Set Up Your Journaling

The Happy Warrior Journal is designed to help you create a life-long journaling practice by giving you a simple framework to process through your feelings and experiences. Heart-centered journaling fosters growth and creates forward movement.

Before Each Session: *Get grounded...*

- **What is your intention for this journaling session?**

  Intention is how you want to feel after a journaling session.

- **What acknowledgements can you give yourself?**

  Start each session by acknowledging a few of your recent accomplishments.

- **Which thoughts have dominated your mind the most?**

  Your thoughts can reflect things that are troubling you or holding you back.

After Each Session: *Reflect….*

- **What Affirmation would help you grow from this journaling session?**

  Affirmations are the positive statements that you use to foster self-belief.

- **What Insights did you have?**

  Insights are the "a-ha" moments that you have while you are journaling.

- **What Habits do you need to change?**

  Habits are recurring ritual practices you design to move your life forward.

- **What Actions do you need to take?**

  Actions are the one-time items that you design to move your life forward?

How to Use the S.E.L.F. Practice

Excerpt from the book, Happy Warrior

One way to strengthen your journaling and doodling is to incorporate the S.E.L.F. practice. S.E.L.F. is the practice of opening yourself up, creating awareness about who you are, and shifting your perspective to become who you want to be.

By employing the four steps of S.E.L.F., you slowly begin to dismantle the old identification with your triggers, patterns, false stories, and self-limiting beliefs. Each time you work through the S.E.L.F. practice, you are creating new, more open, and energizing pathways to elevate your consciousness and Free Your Mind.

The S.E.L.F. practice, as outlined below, is designed to help you process through any feelings you may be having and Choose Love instead of Fear. By making the S.E.L.F. practice into a habit, you will have tools at your disposal whenever you need to re-energize, refocus, and move through anything holding you back.

The S.E.L.F. Practice:

- Stop: Breathe - Take a moment to simply notice your thoughts and feelings.

- Explore - What are the feelings, patterns, and false stories you are noticing?

- Let Go - Be willing to let go of these thoughts and feelings by affirming yourself and acknowledging that you are enough, exactly as you are.

- Free Your Mind - By releasing your attachment to the feelings and false stories, you are creating more freedom in your mind, body, and spirit.

Repeat as often as needed.

Free Your Mind

S.E.L.F. Reflections

When you sit down to journal and/or doodle, take a moment to reflect on the four steps of the S.E.L.F. practice. This will give you a good starting point and a clear intention for your session. It will also help you to walk away with more awareness, clarity, and perspective. Most importantly it will help you to Choose Love.

Benefits of Journaling & Doodling

- **Strengthen Your Internal Journey:** Journaling and Doodling invoke Mindfulness and help you to remain present while shifting your perspective. They provide clarity and help you to gain a greater sense of confidence and self- identity.

- **Think in Big-Pictures:** When you are too focused on drama and details, you can overthink. Journaling and Doodling help you to get out of your thoughts, take a step back and focus on the bigger picture.

- **Reduce Your Stress:** Journaling and Doodling calm anxiety and reduce the negative impact of stress on your mental and physical health.

- **Boost Your Mood:** Journaling and Doodling can improve your mood and give you a greater sense of overall emotional well- being and happiness.

- **Keep Your Brain Sharp:** Journaling and Doodling help boost memory, focus, and comprehension and improve cognitive processing.

SO, IT BEGINS...

S.E.L.F. Reflections - Doodle   Date: /   /

Notes from Yourself:

Once you see, you cannot unsee.

Love, Yourself

S.E.L.F. Reflections - Journal   Date: /   /

S.E.L.F. Reflections - Doodle   Date: /   /

Notes from Yourself:

You can do anything, once you commit to it.

Love, Yourself

S.E.L.F. Reflections - Journal   Date: /   /

_____
_____
_____
_____
_____
_____
_____
_____
_____
_____
_____
_____
_____
_____
_____
_____
_____
_____
_____
_____
_____
_____
_____
_____
_____
_____
_____
_____
_____
_____
_____
_____
_____
_____
_____

S.E.L.F. Reflections - Doodle   Date: /   /

Notes from Yourself:

It all goes back to the setup. Without proper setup, you will run into snags

Love, Yourself

S.E.L.F. Reflections - Journal   Date: /   /

_____
_____
_____
_____
_____
_____
_____
_____
_____
_____
_____
_____
_____
_____
_____
_____
_____
_____
_____
_____
_____
_____
_____
_____
_____
_____
_____
_____
_____
_____
_____

S.E.L.F. Reflections - Doodle   Date: /   /

Notes from Yourself:

Journaling is a practice designed to help you engage your mind, clarify
your vision, and take your life to the next level. You got this!

Love, Yourself

S.E.L.F. Reflections - Journal   Date: /   /

_____
_____
_____
_____
_____
_____
_____
_____
_____
_____
_____
_____
_____
_____
_____
_____
_____
_____
_____
_____
_____
_____
_____
_____
_____
_____
_____
_____
_____
_____
_____
_____
_____
_____

S.E.L.F. Reflections - Doodle   Date: /   /

Notes from Yourself:

*Every area of your life is connected. You can't
focus on one area without impacting the others.*

Love, Yourself

S.E.L.F. Reflections - Journal   *Date: /   /*

S.E.L.F. Reflections - Doodle   Date: /   /

Notes from Yourself:

You are whoever you say you are. Be a badass.

Love, Yourself

S.E.L.F. Reflections - Journal   Date: /   /

S.E.L.F. Reflections - Doodle   Date: /   /

Notes from Yourself:

Every strength is a weakness. Every weakness is a strength.
They are one and the same.

Love, Yourself

S.E.L.F. Reflections - Journal   Date: /   /

_____

_____

_____

_____

_____

_____

_____

_____

_____

_____

_____

_____

_____

_____

_____

_____

_____

_____

_____

_____

_____

_____

_____

_____

_____

_____

_____

_____

_____

_____

_____

_____

S.E.L.F. Reflections - Doodle   Date: /   /

Notes from Yourself:

What makes you tick? What's your "true north?"

Love, Yourself

S.E.L.F. Reflections - Journal   Date: /   /

_____

_____

_____

_____

_____

_____

_____

_____

_____

_____

_____

_____

_____

_____

_____

_____

_____

_____

_____

_____

_____

_____

_____

_____

_____

_____

_____

_____

_____

_____

_____

_____

_____

_____

_____

S.E.L.F. Reflections - Doodle   Date: /   /

Notes from Yourself:

There's a wise little voice inside. Trust it.

Love, Yourself

S.E.L.F. Reflections - Journal   Date: /   /

S.E.L.F. Reflections - Doodle   Date: /   /

Notes from Yourself:

Everything is energy. Use it wisely.

Love, Yourself

S.E.L.F. Reflections - Journal   Date: /   /

S.E.L.F. Reflections - Doodle   Date: /   /

Notes from Yourself:

Saying "yes" to one thing means saying "no" to something else.

Love, Yourself

S.E.L.F. Reflections - Journal   Date: /   /

S.E.L.F. Reflections - Doodle   Date: /   /

Notes from Yourself:

Feelings are temporary. Let them pass through you.

Love, Yourself

S.E.L.F. Reflections - Journal   Date: /   /

_____

_____

_____

_____

_____

_____

_____

_____

_____

_____

_____

_____

_____

_____

_____

_____

_____

_____

_____

_____

_____

_____

_____

_____

_____

_____

_____

_____

_____

_____

_____

_____

S.E.L.F. Reflections - Doodle   Date: /   /

Notes from Yourself:

You are not your thoughts; you are the observer of your thoughts.

Love, Yourself

S.E.L.F. Reflections - Journal   Date: /   /

S.E.L.F. Reflections - Doodle   Date: /   /

Notes from Yourself:

Are you on a mental hamster wheel? What keeps it spinning?

Love, Yourself

S.E.L.F. Reflections - Journal   Date: /   /

_____
_____
_____
_____
_____
_____
_____
_____
_____
_____
_____
_____
_____
_____
_____
_____
_____
_____
_____
_____
_____
_____
_____
_____
_____
_____
_____
_____
_____
_____
_____
_____
_____

S.E.L.F. Reflections - Doodle   Date: /   /

Notes from Yourself:

You have the power to shift your mindset. Shift your thoughts; change your life.

Love, Yourself

S.E.L.F. Reflections - Journal   Date: /   /

S.E.L.F. Reflections - Doodle   Date: /   /

Notes from Yourself:

Find the stillness behind your thoughts, and watch the answers bubble up.

Love, Yourself

S.E.L.F. Reflections - Journal   Date: /   /

_____

_____

_____

_____

_____

_____

_____

_____

_____

_____

_____

_____

_____

_____

_____

_____

_____

_____

_____

_____

_____

_____

_____

_____

_____

_____

_____

_____

S.E.L.F. Reflections - Doodle   Date: /   /

Notes from Yourself:

Don't believe everything you tell yourself. Not all thoughts are created equal.

Love, Yourself

S.E.L.F. Reflections - Journal   Date: /   /

_____
_____
_____
_____
_____
_____
_____
_____
_____
_____
_____
_____
_____
_____
_____
_____
_____
_____
_____
_____
_____
_____
_____
_____
_____
_____
_____
_____
_____
_____
_____
_____

S.E.L.F. Reflections - Doodle   Date: /   /

Notes from Yourself:

You're the author of your life. Write your own story.

Love, Yourself

S.E.L.F. Reflections - Journal   Date: /   /

S.E.L.F. Reflections - Doodle   Date: /   /

Notes from Yourself:

Free your mind, and the rest will follow.

Love, Yourself

S.E.L.F. Reflections - Journal   Date: /   /

S.E.L.F. Reflections - Doodle   Date: /   /

Notes from Yourself:

Let go of what no longer works to create space for what does.

Love, Yourself

S.E.L.F. Reflections - Journal   Date: /   /

_____
_____
_____
_____
_____
_____
_____
_____
_____
_____
_____
_____
_____
_____
_____
_____
_____
_____
_____
_____
_____
_____
_____
_____
_____
_____
_____
_____
_____
_____
_____
_____
_____

S.E.L.F. Reflections - Doodle   Date: /   /

Notes from Yourself:

Rituals are the anchors... that keep your life from floating away.

Love, Yourself

S.E.L.F. Reflections - Journal   Date: /   /

_____
_____
_____
_____
_____
_____
_____
_____
_____
_____
_____
_____
_____
_____
_____
_____
_____
_____
_____
_____
_____
_____
_____
_____
_____
_____
_____
_____
_____
_____
_____
_____
_____

S.E.L.F. Reflections - Doodle   *Date: /   /*

Notes from Yourself:

Where ya goin' beautiful? How you gonna get there?

Love, Yourself

S.E.L.F. Reflections - Journal   Date: /   /

_____
_____
_____
_____
_____
_____
_____
_____
_____
_____
_____
_____
_____
_____
_____
_____
_____
_____
_____
_____
_____
_____
_____
_____
_____
_____
_____
_____
_____
_____
_____
_____
_____

S.E.L.F. Reflections - Doodle   Date: /   /

Notes from Yourself:

Goals are just habits you've shown up for.

Love, Yourself

S.E.L.F. Reflections - Journal   Date: /   /

S.E.L.F. Reflections - Doodle   *Date: /   /*

Notes from Yourself:

Break it down.... one step at a time.

Love, Yourself

S.E.L.F. Reflections - Journal   Date: /   /

_____
_____
_____
_____
_____
_____
_____
_____
_____
_____
_____
_____
_____
_____
_____
_____
_____
_____
_____
_____
_____
_____
_____
_____
_____
_____
_____
_____
_____
_____
_____

S.E.L.F. Reflections - Doodle   Date: /   /

Notes from Yourself:

Your body is your vehicle. Regular service is required.

Love, Yourself

S.E.L.F. Reflections - Journal   Date: /   /

S.E.L.F. Reflections - Doodle   Date: /   /

Notes from Yourself:

Focus on what you love, and happiness will follow.

Love, Yourself

S.E.L.F. Reflections - Journal   Date: /   /

S.E.L.F. Reflections - Doodle   Date: /   /

Notes from Yourself:

Life is about learning to love yourself and others.

Love, Yourself

S.E.L.F. Reflections - Journal   Date: /   /

_____
_____
_____
_____
_____
_____
_____
_____
_____
_____
_____
_____
_____
_____
_____
_____
_____
_____
_____
_____
_____
_____
_____
_____
_____
_____
_____
_____
_____
_____
_____
_____
_____
_____
_____

S.E.L.F. Reflections - Doodle   Date: /   /

Notes from Yourself:

Surround yourself with beauty and do things you love.

Love, Yourself

S.E.L.F. Reflections - Journal   Date: /   /

S.E.L.F. Reflections - Doodle   Date: /   /

Notes from Yourself:

If you can see it, you can be it.

Love, Yourself

S.E.L.F. Reflections - Journal   Date: /   /

S.E.L.F. Reflections - Doodle   Date: /   /

Notes from Yourself:

Ask yourself, "what can I give?" Instead of, "what can I get?"

Love, Yourself

S.E.L.F. Reflections - Journal   Date: /   /

_____
_____
_____
_____
_____
_____
_____
_____
_____
_____
_____
_____
_____
_____
_____
_____
_____
_____
_____
_____
_____
_____
_____
_____
_____
_____
_____
_____
_____
_____
_____
_____
_____
_____
_____
_____

S.E.L.F. Reflections - Doodle   Date: /   /

Notes from Yourself:

Every ending... is just another beginning.

Love, Yourself

S.E.L.F. Reflections - Journal   Date: /   /

Want More?

The *Happy Warrior Journal* and *Happy Warrior ~ Your Practical Guide to a Happy Life,* are powered by Selfscription®. These books are designed to help you Free Your Mind and take your life to the next level. Selfscription® also has additional products and services to guide you on your happiness journey:

- Happy Warrior ~ Your Practical Guide to a Happy Life
- Reflection Journal
- Pocket Planner
- Meeting Book
- Session Book
- 1:1 Coaching

To check out our products please visit Amazon.com/Selfscription.

Work with a life coach, stay in the loop on other products and services, and receive inspiring articles, updates, and offers by signing up at Selfscription.com.

Exclusive Offer for Happy Warriors: Mention your Happy Warrior Journal and receive one free coaching session with the purchase of any 9 or 18-session coaching package. Book your complimentary consultation today at Selfscription.com

Choose Love,

John & Jami

If found, please return to:

Name: _____

Phone: _____

Email: _____

www.ingramcontent.com/pod-product-compliance
Lightning Source LLC
Chambersburg PA
CBHW062008090426
42811CB00005B/790